THE DIETRICH VON HILDEBRAND
LIFEGUIDE

The Dietrich von Hildebrand LifeGuide

Dietrich von Hildebrand

Edited by Jules van Schaijik

A LifeGuide™ Series Title

ST. AUGUSTINE'S PRESS
South Bend, Indiana
in association with
the Dietrich von Hildebrand Legacy Project

3 4 5 6   23 22 21 20 10 18 17 16

Library of Congress Cataloging in Publication
Von Hildebrand, Dietrich, 1889–
[Selections. English]
The Dietrich von Hildebrand lifeguide / Dietrich
von Hildebrand; edited by Jules van Schaijik.
p. cm.—(LifeGuide series)
Includes bibliographical references and index.
ISBN 978-1-58731-179-6 (paperbound: alk. paper)
1. Catholic Church—Doctrines. 2. Theology.
I. Van Schaijik, Jules. II. Title.
BX1751.3.V6613 2007
230'.2–dc22   2007007171

∞ The paper used in this publication meets the
minimum requirements of the American National
Standard for Information Sciences—Permanence of
Paper for Printed Materials, ANSI Z39.48-1984.

St. Augustine's Press
www.staugustine.net

Contents

Dietrich von Hildebrand 1889–1977

Dietrich von Hildebrand was an original philosopher, religious writer, heroic anti-Nazi activist, courageous Christian witness, and passionate proponent of beauty and culture.

Born in 1889 as the son of a famous German sculptor, von Hildebrand grew up in the rich artistic setting of Florence and Munich. He studied philosophy under Edmund Husserl, the founder of phenomenology and a giant of twentieth century philosophy, and under Adolf Reinach, and was profoundly influenced by his close friend, German philosopher Max Scheler, who helped to pave the way for his conversion to Catholicism in 1914.

By 1930 von Hildebrand had become an important voice in German Catholicism, perhaps best known for his pioneering work on man and woman and on marriage. One can trace the chapter on marriage in *Gaudium et spes* of Vatican II back to von Hildebrand's writings in the 20's in which he argued that the marital act has not only a procreative meaning but a no less significant unitive meaning. But he also distinguished himself in other ways during his years at the University of Munich, most of all through his ethical writings and through his book, *The Metaphysics of Community*, in which he used the resources of phenomenology to rethink fundamental issues of social philosophy and of moral philosophy.

When Hitler came to power in 1933, von Hildebrand left his native Germany, and dedicated himself to resisting Nazism. He moved to Vienna and founded a journal for combating at the level of philosophical first principles the rising Nazi ideology and for defending the independence of Austria against Germany. With the German occupation of Austria in 1938, von Hildebrand became a political fugitive; fleeing through Czechoslovakia, Switzerland, France, Portugal, and Brazil, he eventually arrived in the United States in 1940.

Von Hildebrand wrote many works unfolding the faith and morals of Catholicism, such as *In Defense of Purity*, *Marriage*, *Liturgy and Personality*, and, above all, *Transformation in Christ*, now recognized as a classic of Christian spirituality.

In the United States von Hildebrand taught at Fordham University until his retirement in 1959. Many of his most important philosophical works—among them *Ethics*, *What is Philosophy?*, *The Nature of Love*, *Morality and Situation Ethics*, *The Heart*, and *Aesthetics*—were completed in the United States.

Through his many writings, von Hildebrand contributed to the development of a rich Christian personalism, which in many ways converges with that of Karol Wojtyla/Pope John Paul II.

Von Hildebrand died in New Rochelle NY in 1977.

Preface

With a literary corpus as large and varied as that of Dietrich von Hildebrand, the editor of a brief anthology is faced with the challenge of finding a principle of selection that can enable him to give the reader not just a series of insightful passages but a sense of the essence of the man and of the general thrust of his contributions to Catholic thought and culture. Of particular concern to me was to try to show what I have felt more deeply the more I have studied von Hildebrand, namely, that while his work has an unmistakable classical air, he was, eminently, a man of our time and for our time. This comes through clearly in what could be called von Hildebrand's *personalist emphasis*.

In his introduction to *The New Tower of Babel*, a collection of essays in which he examines various manifestations of modern man's flight from God, von Hildebrand wrote that "[t]he dignity of the human person is written over this period as its objective theme, regardless of how few persons hold the right and valid notion of this dignity and its metaphysical basis. The present epoch is great because the struggle that centers around the human person is ultimately a fight engaged under the banner of Christ . . . "

This great struggle "centered around the human person" and engaged "under the banner of Christ" provides an interpretive key to the life and work of Dietrich von Hildebrand. Whether it was his heroic resistance to the evil of totalitarianism, or his critique of relativism, materialism, and all secularizing trends; his value ethics, his personalist metaphysics, his emphasis on the heart, the liturgy, beauty, marriage and love; whether in his religious writings or his philosophical writings, his teaching in the classroom or in the small gatherings of friends and disciples in his grand home in Munich or in his tiny New York apartment, his passion and the implicit mission of his life was to unfold, cherish, and defend the great mystery of what it means to be a human person—a being called to live his life in conscious, free, and full responsiveness to the world of values and above all to God, who created him, who redeemed him, and who offers him total transformation in Christ.

It is his dedication to this great theme, too, which perhaps accounts for the remarkable accessibility of von Hildebrand's thought. Though he deals in deepest philosophical truths at the highest levels of intellectual seriousness and originality, he is never arcane or dryly academic. He manages to engage the minds and hearts of "ordinary" readers, because he addresses himself not to "interesting problems," but to the deepest yearnings and aspirations of our hearts, and to the concrete questions perplexing our minds. What is the meaning of human life? Is my longing for love nothing but naïve sentimentality or selfishness? Is it possible to know Truth? Is there such a thing as greatness? Can my life be changed, even now?

This is not to say that von Hildebrand is always easy to read. Certainly, many of his most important contributions are well beyond the purview of the present format. (These deserve much more scholarly attention than they have yet received.) My purpose here is only to give a kind of foretaste: a feel for the personality of von Hildebrand, the nobility of his spirit, and the greatness of his thought, by selecting passages that reveal it best—passages I find particularly compelling and particularly *apropos* today.

Jules van Schaijik
October, 2006

Truth

It seems fitting to begin this anthology of Dietrich von Hildebrand, that ardent lover of truth, with a passage on the importance of truth for human life and interpersonal communion. It is taken from an essay in which he criticizes "one of the most ominous features of the present epoch" which, he thinks, is "undoubtedly the dethronement of truth."

The role of truth in human life is so predominant and so decisive, the interest in the question of whether a thing is true or not is so indispensable in all the domains of human life (ranging from the most humble everyday affairs to the highest spiritual spheres), that the dethronement of truth entails the decomposition of man's very life.

Disrespect for truth—when not merely a theoretical thesis, but a lived attitude—patently destroys all morality, even all reasonability and all community life. All objective norms are dissolved by this attitude of indifference toward truth; so also is the possibility of resolving any discussion or controversy objectively. Peace among individuals or nations and all trust in other persons are impossible as well. The very basis of a really human life is subverted. . . .

There exists an intimate link between the

dethronement of truth and terrorism. As soon as man no longer refers to truth as the ultimate judge in all spheres of life, brutal force necessarily replaces right; oppression and mechanical, suggestive influence supersedes conviction; fear supplants trust.

Indeed, to dethrone truth means to sever the human person from the very basis of his spiritual existence; it is the most radical, practical atheism and thus is deeply linked with the depersonalization of man, the anti-personalism that is the characteristic feature of Communism and of all the different types of totalitarianism. An abyss separates this decomposition of human life and of the human person from the attitude expressed in the words of St. Augustine: "O Truth, Truth, how inwardly did the very marrow of my soul pant for you."[1]

Von Hildebrand is by no means the first philosopher to draw attention to the fact that our understanding of the world, especially that of its deeper dimensions, depends not only on the acuity of our intellect but also on the rectitude of our will. What is unique, however, is the depth and originality with which he has analyzed this issue. One of his earliest works, for instance, is dedicated entirely to the problem of culpable "value-blindness" in the moral sphere. What follows is a passage in which von Hildebrand describes the way in which certain fundamental moral attitudes hinder a true and deep understanding of reality.

In the first place we find *indolence*. I do not mean here that peripheral indolence which keeps man from any intellectual labor (*laziness* so-called) but I mean . . .

the indolence that renders any real penetration of the object impossible and prevents any collaboration with the meaning and essence of a thing.

Certain kinds of things . . . require for their apprehension a certain *élan* of the whole man, a kind of soaring power of the mind, a willingness to abandon a customary attitude and to look in a new direction, and, above all, to allow oneself to be carried along by the spirit of the object in question and to "collaborate," to "conspire" with it.

But indolence, which is anchored deep down in the concupiscence of man and involves a passivity, a strange, dull insistence on remaining rooted to the spot one is accustomed to, closes whole stretches of reality to the intellectual vision. As long as we remain in this attitude of central indolence, no intellectual acumen, no abundance of erudition, no merely formal capacity of apprehension can open our eyes to the understanding of the deeper strata and connections of existing things, or of higher kinds of objects of knowledge. . . .

Another fundamental attitude darkening the understanding is the incapacity, rooted in pride, to listen, to let things themselves speak, to allow them to instruct us. What I mean here is that pedagogic pedantry in the face of the world which destroys all wonder which, according to Plato, is the beginning of all true knowledge. There are people who approach things . . . without the respectful desire to penetrate them with real understanding, without any thirst for truth, but rather with a supercilious repletion and an obtuse smugness that renders open-mindedness impossible. People of that kind are blind . . . to all the things that constitute the height and the depth of the world. . . .

Worse still is the attitude of definite resentment which rebels against the objectivity and autonomy of things and especially against the existence of objective values. It resents being bound by an objective validity. It prevents any real friendship with an object, any willingness to listen to the voice of things, and it does so, not as a conscious gesture, but—much worse—as an unconscious fundamental attitude. . . .

This attitude prevents any illumination because at bottom it does not want to be illuminated. This is the attitude of the radical skeptic . . . or that of the relativist who repeats with deep satisfaction the absurd thesis of the relativity of all values. With such minds no arguments are of the slightest use, however convincing they may be: minds of this sort will not admit the convincing power of argument. Only the abandonment of their fundamental attitude, only a conversion, a relaxing of the grip of their pride, can give them sight and lead to a liberation of their intellect. . . .

Finally, there is a fundamental attitude of lack of spirit, of *distrust* toward things, which disturbs the understanding and condemns it to impotence. I mean here that constitutional distrust which renders a man incapable of understanding the simplest set of facts, because he cannot muster the necessary courage to entrust himself to the object and because it seems to him an act of rashness to reach a definite conclusion at any point whatever. Perpetually he refers the decision to a further court of appeal, and avoids a definite *Yes* or *No* even in the most obvious situations.

This attitude in the intellectual sphere corresponds in the moral sphere to the running away from every responsibility. . . . [2]

Conversely, a good fundamental attitude opens our minds to receive reality.

[T]he specifically Catholic attitude to the world of reality . . . is precisely the fundamental attitude that *delivers* our knowledge, clears away all the fetters and hindrances to knowledge, and so produces the type of mind capable of doing justice to the depth and range of reality. The Catholic attitude is specifically open-minded, specifically anti-pedantic, anti-self-compla-cent, soaring, and filled with respect for reality. . . .

. . . [T]he true Catholic attitude is one of humil-ity, free from all resentment, ready to submit and to serve; it is metaphysically courageous, healthy, undis-gruntled, *believing*. I say this is the *Catholic attitude*, *not* the attitude of the average Catholic. We may indeed be told, not without justification, that many Catholic men of science and erudition show a lack of this attitude more than many non-Catholics. If we think of some of the great men of antiquity (such as Socrates, Plato, and Aristotle) or those of modern times (such as Kepler, Newton, Robert Mayer, Leibnitz, and Humboldt), we find that they were, in their fundamental attitude, far more *Catholic* than many a Catholic. How much smugness and pedantry, how much metaphysical indolence do we not find among Catholics and Catholic thinkers and men of science! Certainly. But not because they are Catholics; rather because they are *not Catholic enough*, because their attitude has not been formed by dogma, because dogma has not become the principle of their life, so that the attitude they display does not fully correspond with what they affirm in their Faith. Where, on the contrary, this is the case (as with St. Augustine, St. Anselm, St. Bonaventure, St. Albertus Magnus, St. Thomas Aquinas, Pascal, Père Gratry, Cardinal Newman, Giambattista Rossi, Vico, Toniolo, and Pasteur), there we also find that fundamental attitude which delivers knowledge and opens the way for it.[3]

The above insights, among others, lead von Hildebrand to call for genuinely Catholic universities, in which professors are free in both the academic and the moral sense, precisely in order to further a true and adequate understanding of reality.

Catholic universities are therefore necessary for the sake of truly adequate objective knowledge, not by any means merely for the protection of the religious convictions of the students. They are needed as the institutions where Catholic thinkers and men of science, supported by a truly Catholic environment, informed in their attitude by the spirit of Christ and of His Church, shall be enabled by a really unbiased, truly liberated and enlightened intelligence to penetrate adequately into reality and to achieve by organized teamwork that *universitas* which in these days is so urgently needed.

They must further be institutions in which young people may be educated to that attitude which also represents an inevitable prerequisite for the learner. A Catholic university would have no meaning if it were nothing but a collection of Catholic men of thought and science, while following the model of the modern university in its general atmosphere. It requires the conscious production of an atmosphere filled by Christ, an environment imbued with prayer. As an organism it must, in its structure and in the common life of its teachers among each other and with their students, be thoroughly Catholic. The students must breathe a Catholic air and Catholic spirit which will make them into anti-pedantic, humble, faithful, and metaphysically courageous men of winged intelligence and yearning, and therewith capable of truly adequate and objective knowledge. The demand for a Catholic university must therefore be pressed in the name of such adequate knowledge and not by any means only in the interest of Catholics.[4]

Value

Underlying all of von Hildebrand's thought lies a distinction between two radically different kinds of goods (or "importance," as he likes to say), a distinction implicitly recognized by all great thinkers but analyzed by von Hildebrand with unsurpassed clarity and originality. It is the distinction between those things which are intrinsically *valuable, that is, valuable simply because of what they are in themselves and thus apart from any relation they may have to us (such as a human person, an act of forgiveness, or a beautiful painting), and those things we call good merely because they are in some way agreeable to us, because they satisfy our desires (such as a comfortable chair) or gratify our pride (such as a flattering remark). In the following passages von Hildebrand draws out the most important contrasts between these different types of "good" and also shows how relevant they are for understanding the life of the person.*

Let us begin . . . by comparing the two following experiences:

In the first, let us suppose that someone pays us a compliment. We are perhaps aware that we do not fully deserve it, but it is nevertheless an agreeable and pleasurable experience. . . . It presents itself as agreeable and as possessing the character of a *bonum*, in short, as something important.

In the second, let us suppose that we witness a generous action, a man's forgiveness of a grave injury. This again strikes us as distinguishable from the neutral activity of a man dressing himself or lighting a cigarette. Indeed, the act of generous forgiveness shines forth with the mark of importance, with the mark of something noble and precious. It moves us and engenders our admiration. We are not only aware that this act occurs, but that it is *better* that it occurs, *better* that the man acted in this way rather than in another. We are conscious that this act is something which *ought* to *be*, something *important*.

If we compare these types of importance, we will soon discover the essential difference between them. The first, that is, the compliment, is merely *subjectively* important; while the latter, the act of forgiving, is *important in itself*. We are fully conscious that the compliment possesses a character of importance only insofar as it gives us pleasure. Its importance is solely drawn from its relation to our pleasure—as soon as the compliment is divorced from our pleasure, it sinks back into the anonymity of the neutral and indifferent.

In contrast, the generous act of forgiveness presents itself as something intrinsically important. We are clearly conscious that its importance in no way depends on any effect which it produces in us. Its particular importance is not drawn from any relation to our pleasure and satisfaction. It stands before us as intrinsically and autonomously important, in no way dependent on any relation to our reaction. . . .

The intrinsic importance with which a generous act of forgiveness is endowed is termed "value," as distinguished from the importance of all those goods which motivate our interest merely because they are agreeable or satisfactory to us. [5]

The difference between value and the merely subjectively satisfying becomes even clearer when we consider the way in which they are related to pleasure and happiness. True happiness, von Hildebrand shows, is the result of conforming

*ourselves to what is intrinsically valuable. This happiness
cannot be directly willed, but rather follows from a life
lived in harmony with the world of values.*

But, although these two types of importance are
essentially different, are they not in another respect
quite similar? Is it not true that those things which
are good, beautiful, noble, or sublime deeply touch
us, fill us with joy and delight? Certainly they do not
leave us indifferent. . . . Yet an analysis of the specific character of delight will prove still more clearly
the essential difference between these two kinds of
importance. It will prove that the value possesses its
importance independently of its effect on us.

The delight and emotion which we experience in
witnessing a noble moral action or in gazing at the
beauty of a star-studded sky essentially presupposes
the consciousness that the importance of the object
is in no way dependent on the delight it may bestow
on us. Indeed, this bliss arises from our confrontation with an object having an intrinsic importance;
an object standing majestically before us, autonomous in its sublimity and nobility. Our bliss implies
in fact that here is an object which depends in no way
on our reaction to it, an object whose importance we
cannot alter, which we can neither increase nor
diminish: for it draws its importance not from its
relation to us, but from its own rank; it stands before
us, a message, as it were, from on high, elevating us
beyond ourselves.

Thus, this difference between the bliss emanating
from the sheer existence of a value and the pleasure

accruing from the subjectively satisfying is itself not a difference of degree, but a difference of kind: an essential difference. A life which consisted in a continuous stream of pleasures, as derived from what is merely subjectively satisfying, could never grant us one moment of that blissful happiness engendered by those objects possessing a value.

. . . Self-centered happiness at length wears itself out and ends in boredom and emptiness, the constant enjoyment of the merely subjectively satisfying finally throws us back upon our own limitedness, imprisoning us within ourselves.

In contrast, our engagement with a value elevates us, liberates us from self-centeredness, reposes us in a transcendent order which is independent of us, of our moods, of our dispositions. This blissful experience presupposes a participation in the intrinsically important; it implies a harmony which is given forth by the intrinsically good, the essentially noble alone; and it displays to us a brightness which is "consubstantial" (congenial) with the intrinsic beauty and splendor of the value. In this priceless contact with the intrinsically and autonomously important, the important in itself, it is the object which shelters and embraces our spirit.

In the Prologue to Wagner's opera *Tannhäuser*, that is, in the Venusberg scene, we see Tannhäuser longing to break through the circle of a life which affords one pleasure after another. He would prefer even noble suffering to his self-imprisonment. Here we witness some elements of this longing for something important in itself to which alone we can "abandon" ourselves in the true sense of the word. It is indeed a deep characteristic of man to desire to be confronted with something beyond self-centeredness, which obligates us and affords us the possibility of transcending the limits of our subjective inclinations, tendencies, urges, and drives rooted *exclusively* in our nature.

In effect, then, we can say that both the value and the subjectively satisfying can delight us. But it is precisely the *nature* of this delight which clearly reveals the essential difference between the two kinds of goods. The true, profound happiness which the values effect in us necessarily implies an awareness of the object's intrinsic importance. This happiness is essentially an epiphenomenon, for it is in no way the root of this importance, but flows superabundantly out of it. The consciousness that a generous act of forgiveness possesses its importance independently, whether or not I know of its existence, whether or not I rejoice about it, is at the very root of the happiness we experience when confronted with it. This happiness is thus something secondary, notwithstanding the fact that it is an essential mark of the values to be able to bestow delight on us: we even *should* take delight in them. The value is here the *principium* (the determining) and our happiness, the *principiatum* (the determined), whereas in the case of the subjectively satisfying good our pleasure is the *principium* and the importance of the agreeable or satisfying of the object, the *principiatum*.[6]

A third important contrast between value and the merely

subjectively satisfying is revealed when we look at the precise way in which they appeal to our will and affections. In one case, our free spiritual center is awakened and challenged, while in the other it tends to be bypassed and lulled to sleep.

A further distinguishing mark is to be found in the way in which each type of importance addresses itself to us. Every good possessing a value imposes on us, as it were, an obligation to give to it an adequate response. We are not yet referring to the unique obligation which we call moral obligation and which appeals to our conscience. This obligation issues from certain values only. Here we are thinking of the awareness which we have as soon as we are confronted with something intrinsically important, for instance, with beauty in nature or in art, with the majesty of a great truth, with the splendor of moral values. In all these cases we are clearly aware that the object calls for an adequate response. We grasp that it is not left to our arbitrary decision or to our accidental mood whether we respond or not, and how we respond. On the other hand, goods which are merely subjectively satisfying address no such call to us. They attract us or invite us, but we are clearly aware that no response is due to them, that it is up to us whether we heed their invitation or not. When a delectable dish attracts us, we are quite aware that it is completely up to our mood whether or not we yield to this attraction. We all know how ridiculous it would be for someone to say that he submitted to the obligation of playing bridge, and overcame the temptation to assist a sick person.

The call of an authentic value for an adequate response addresses itself to us in a sovereign but non-intrusive, sober way. It appeals to our free spiritual center. The attraction of the subjectively satisfying, on the contrary, lulls us into a state where we yield to instinct; it tends to dethrone our free spiritual center. Its appeal is insistent, oftentimes assuming the character of a temptation, trying to sway and silence our conscience, taking hold of us in an obtrusive manner. Far different is the call of values: it has no obtrusive character; it speaks to us from above, and at a sober distance; it speaks with an objective vigor, issuing a majestic call which we cannot alter by our wishes. [7]

Last but not least, the difference between value and the merely subjectively satisfying is reflected in the way in which we respond to them. In a genuine response to value we transcend ourselves, while in seeking out the merely agreeable we remain centered on ourselves.

[A] decisive mark of the value response is its character of self-abandonment. In enthusiasm, veneration, love, or adoration, we break open our self-centeredness and conform to the important-in-itself. Our interest in the object is completely based on and completely nourished by the intrinsic goodness, beauty and preciousness of the object, and the mysterious rhythm of its intrinsic importance. The value response is, therefore, essentially a conforming of ourselves to the *logos* of the value. The very nature of the inner movement of the value response consists in partaking in the rhythm of the values. . . .

. . . In desiring the merely subjectively satisfying, there is no transcending of the frame of self-centeredness, no conforming to that which is objectively important, no self-abandonment, no reverent submission to something greater than ourselves; on the contrary, there is only imprisonment in the frame of our self-centeredness. . . .

Every response motivated by the merely subjectively satisfying implies a gesture toward the good in question directed toward its appropriation. The object thus appropriated is considered as something which will be sacrificed to us. . . . The value response, on the other hand, is characterized by an element of respect for the good, an interest in its integrity and existence as such, a giving of ourselves to it instead of a consuming of it.[8]

The importance of intrinsic values and our ability to respond to them can hardly be overstated.

The capacity to transcend himself is one of man's deepest characteristics. So long as we consider his activities as the mere unfolding of his entelechy, determined by his nature, or as immanent manifestations of principles proper to his nature, we fail to grasp the most decisive feature of his character as a person. Man cannot be understood if we interpret all his activities as manifestations of an automatic striving for self-perfection. So long as we are confined to this pattern, so long as we see man differing from other beings only by the fact that their objective teleological tendency assumes in him a character of consciousness, we overlook the real nature of man as a person. It is not an immanent movement, unconscious or conscious, which is man's typical mark. Certainly this also is to be found in man's nature, in the physiological sphere as well as in the psychical. But the specifically personal character of man as a subject manifests itself in his capacity to transcend himself. This transcendence displays itself above all in participation in the objective *logos* of being which takes place in knowledge insofar as our intellect conforms itself to the nature of the object, and which again takes place in every value response wherein we conform either with our will or with our heart to the important-in-itself. This kind of participation is absolutely impossible for any impersonal being.[9]

Once the true nature of values and their ennobling effect on the human person has been clearly seen, it follows that they should have a central place in the education and formation of the person.

Being affected plays a paramount role in the development of a personality. Through this channel come seduction, moral poisoning, blunting, narrowing, and cramping, as well as moral elevation, purification, enrichment, widening and liberation. For the pedagogue, one of the principal means for moral education is to expose the souls of his pupils to being affected by values. In every effort toward moral and religious progress, this opening of the soul also plays an eminent role.[10]

In being affected by a value, we are broadened

and elevated above ourselves; in being affected by the merely subjectively satisfying, we are rather made narrow and in no way elevated above ourselves. In being affected by values we also experience the unifying power of the values: we become internally more unified, more recollected.[11]

Besides intrinsic values, which possess their goodness apart from any effect they have on us, von Hildebrand also recognizes what he calls "objective goods for the person." Like values, and unlike the merely subjectively satisfying, these goods are objectively and truly good. But their goodness consists in their being somehow conducive to our wellbeing and true happiness. It is important to see, as von Hildebrand repeatedly writes, that it is in no way illegitimate or selfish to be profoundly interested in such goods. On the contrary, it is deeply characteristic and more than proper for persons to be "self-interested" in this sense.

Whoever does not acknowledge the transcendence of human beings fails to understand what distinguishes them as persons from all impersonal creatures. But whoever detects something egocentric in the fact that I desire an objective good for myself, whoever thinks that the ideal of human life is for me to lose all interest in beneficial goods for myself, fails to understand the character of man as subject. He fails to see the mysterious center to which everything in the life of a person is referred, the center that is addressed by beneficial goods and that is inseparably bound up with his dignity as person. If the first error locks persons in themselves and in this way distorts their ultimate relation to the world and to God, the second error deprives them of their character as full selves. The first error reduces man to the biological, taking him according to the model of a plant or animal. The second error robs him of his character as a full subject and destroys the personal in him by exaggerating the objective to the point of dissolving that which makes him a subject.[12]

Von Hildebrand shows further that there is no conflict between this interest in our own wellbeing and happiness and the value-responding attitude. In fact, such legitimate self-interestedness heightens and perfects the value-response. This is very clear, for instance, with regard to our value-responding love of God, in which the desire to be forever united with Him (i.e. the desire for our happiness), plays a significant role.

The full conforming to values, as it is expressed above all in the central response-to-value of love, implies not only the affirmation of the value in itself . . . but also the longing for union with the object of value, the spiritual "hastening" toward the beloved, in which the unique giving up of one's own person is achieved. And just this *full* response-to-value is *due* to God. . . . Otherwise the response-to-value would not be complete. To see a selfish motive behind this longing for union would be to fall victim to a grave error. It would imply the failure to see clearly how this longing grows necessarily out of pure value-responsiveness, and how the giving of oneself can only find its fulfillment in this longing. . . . The liturgy teaches us that this striving [toward union] belongs to the true relationship to God; that, further, the *intentio unionis* is *due* to God; that God demands from us not only adoration but also love; and that He Himself loves us with this love. The longing to touch God, the will to attain to Him, is not only a profoundly legitimate element of the liturgical act, it is even necessary for the full glorification of God. . . .[13]

. . . If this were lacking, then the value-responding affirmation would not be complete and full-blooded, it would be a mere acknowledgement instead of a giving up of oneself.[14]

Our experience of conscience, too, reveals that there is no conflict between the transcendence we achieve in responding to a moral obligation and our own interiority and genuine interest in our integrity and happiness.

A moral call is addressed to someone to intervene in a certain situation; perhaps another is in danger, or perhaps he has to refuse to do some evil which is asked of him. He grasps the morally relevant value, he understands its call, he is aware of the moral obligation, which appeals to his conscience. On the one hand, we have here a high-point of transcendence in the pure commitment to the morally relevant good. But on the other hand, this call, insofar as it is morally obligatory, pre-eminently contains the element of "*tua res agitur*" ("the thing concerns *you* personally"). In a certain sense this call is my most intimate and personal concern, in which I experience the uniqueness of my self. Supreme objectivity and supreme subjectivity interpenetrate here. One can even say that we have here the dramatic highpoint of the "*tua res agitur*" in our earthly existence. On the one hand, I commit myself to something which in no way stands before me as merely an "objective good for me," but rather as something which appeals to me as valuable in itself; but on the other hand, since a moral obligation in its unique impact is here at stake . . . my decision to follow the call or not, eminently reaches into the innermost center of my own existence (*Eigenleben*). When the moral call is addressed to me and appeals to my conscience, then at the same time the question of my own salvation comes up. It is not just the [objective] "issue" which is at stake; I and my salvation are just as much at stake.[15]

Freedom

Von Hildebrand's deep grasp of the nature of the human person, the moral life, and man's relation to God led him to new and profound reflections on the nature and scope of human freedom. The limits of this format prevent the inclusion of many important writings (some of which are too technical for a general audience) on this theme. But here is one on the freedom we have with respect to deep experiences and responses in the soul, which, though not initiated through our freedom, can yet be incorporated by it so as to become fully our own.

There also exists a fundamentally different way in which man's freedom displays itself: the free attitude toward experiences already existing in our soul. We have the freedom of taking a position toward experiences which have come into existence without our free intervention, and which also cannot be dissipated by our free influence. . . . Let us first consider the cooperative role of man's freedom with respect to being affected. We can abandon ourselves to this experience, we can open our soul in its very depth, we can expose our soul to the action of the value; or we can close ourselves, we can abstain from accepting it freely, from letting ourselves be pervaded by it: we can counteract it.

We can freely engender several different attitudes toward our being affected. Above all, with our free center we can say "yes" or "no" to our being affected. Furthermore there is in us the capacity of consciously "drinking" into our soul, as it were, the contents of the object. We can expose our soul to it; we can freely surrender to it; we can let ourselves be permeated by it. These free attitudes deeply modify the experience itself: only in them does it become fully our own.

. . . A great part of morality is concerned with this type of freedom; man is called not only to accomplish moral actions in which something is brought into existence through his will or is destroyed by it, but also to take a free position toward those experiences which exist in him and which he can neither create nor destroy by his will.[16]

Human freedom, von Hildebrand is deeply aware, is a created freedom. This means not only that it is limited in various ways, but also that it is a gift. In the following passage von Hildebrand draws attention to one way in which our most free acts, those we can call in the highest sense "our own" and for which we are in the highest sense responsible, are also paradoxically acts in which we are most dependent on God.

Time and again, certain specific situations may occur—situations, to be sure, that we cannot conjure up at will—in which our free "centre of personality" is given the capacity to bring about, by a single and definite act, a durable transformation of our inmost being. For example, there may be a moment when our renunciation of some cherished good of high intrinsic value will usher in, beyond the limits of our relation to that good, a process of detachment from terrestrial goods in general. There may be cases, again, when our forgiving a person whom we have long held in scorn takes on the form of a softening of heart in a general and in an enduring sense as well. Or again, a deep humiliation may, in given circumstances, start off our wholesale emancipation from our slavery to pride. These are moments in which, thanks to a gift of God, our range of direct power is suddenly extended, so that the effectiveness of our free decision may advance into the depths of our being. . . .

It is not, as has been observed above, in our power to conjure up such situations. These moments, when the operativeness of our freedom is increased and the range of our power expanded to a degree far beyond normal, bear an unmistakable character of gratuitous gifts. Whereas ordinarily we can only posit such free actions as may be supposed to exercise an indirect effect in favor of our transformation, in these supreme moments we may make a decisive forward step concerning our permanent state of soul. It is to these moments that St. Paul refers when he says: "Behold, now is the acceptable time . . . now is the day of salvation." . . . Nor must we allow these decisive moments to pass unused: "Today if you shall hear his voice, harden not your hearts" . . .[17]

In his classic religious work, Transformation in Christ, *von Hildebrand discusses many ways in which man can be "unfree" in a moral sense of the term. The following passage, dealing with the unfreedom caused by a fear of being deemed a fool by others, is one example.*

Fear, in general, is one of the greatest enemies of our freedom—be it the fear of physical danger, the fear of poverty, the fear of incurring somebody's hatred, the fear of becoming an object of people's talk. . . . We shall pass now to a further type of unfreedom, closely akin to the one engendered by fear—the unfreedom due to what is currently termed *human respect.* . . . [I]t is a combination of pride and a sense of insecurity that causes the subject to base his appraisal of self on the image other people may have of him rather than on the picture of himself he may derive from his confrontation with God. In the first place, therefore, he will be anxious not to appear stupid, crack-brained, backward, and in general, ridiculous in the eyes of others. Hence, in many cases, he will shrink from professing his faith before others, dread being seen in church, refrain from crossing himself at table in the presence of unbelievers, and so forth. This type of unfreedom is particularly obnoxious in a Christian. Of course, it will hardly ever occur in such blatant forms in the case of a person who *has* determined to follow Christ unreservedly; but in a more mitigated form, at least, it easily steals into anyone's mental constitution. Yet, the true Christian should be *completely free* from this pitiable dependence on "the world." Knowing that Christ must be "scandal to the world," he should serenely endure being deemed by the world a fool, ridiculous, or narrow-minded. He ought never to forget these words of Christ: "If you had been of the world, the world would love its own: but you are not of the world, but I have chosen you out of the world, therefore, the world hateth you." . . . It is often easier to profess Christ in big things, and even to accept heavy sacrifices for Christ's sake, than to put up with disdain or derision in the humdrum situations of daily life. And yet we should at every moment be ready—and gladly so—to pass for a "fool for Christ's sake." This is not to deny that we do well to avoid in our outward bearing all unnecessary demonstrativeness; to observe certain canons of discretion too often neglected by zealous converts; and to take account of the circumstances, including the degree of susceptibility of those who happen to be present. But this must proceed from a state of inner freedom; from a sovereign attitude of mind rising above the situation. Far from allowing our human respect to make us dependent on the unbelievers' appreciation, or letting our behaviour be determined by their taste and their measures, we must—in joyful readiness to appear, if need be, as "fools for Christ's sake"—be able to decide before God what, with regard to the salvation of the souls of our fellow men, we should do and what we had better omit.[18]

Virtue

To understand the substantiality and depth of the human person, and his continuity with himself through time, it is important to see that he is capable of responses and commitments which go deeper than and outlast the present conscious moment. In the following von Hildebrand shows this, using love as an example.

Love for a person obviously does not cease to exist whenever we are forced to focus our attention on other objects. There is a definite difference between the moments in which we are able to actualize our love fully—perhaps when we speak to the beloved person, or perhaps when we think of him in his absence—and the moments in which we must concentrate on some work or in which a deep sorrow about something else fills our heart. But whereas a pain in my finger is by its very nature restricted in its existence to being actually and consciously experienced, whereas it is situated by its very nature in the stratum of actual experience, the love for another

person continues to exist even if it is not actualized
. . . . Love for another person subsists as a full factor
in my soul, coloring every other situation, deeply
forming my life. It subsists not as any vague subcon-
scious element, but as a meaningful response to the
beloved person. It tends indeed to be actualized, but
in its character of a meaningful response to the
beloved it does not live only on its full actualizations.

This subsistence of certain responses in a stratum
deeper than the one in which the full actualization of
our experiences takes place, shall be termed "superactual existence." There exist several responses
which, by their very nature, are not restricted to a
mere actual experience, but must subsist in a superactual way if they are at all real and not mere sham
acts. The love for a person which is dissipated as
soon as we lose sight of the beloved can not really be
love. It is above all love which has such a superactual character; other responses like wrath, a fit of anger,
or laughing about someone who is comical cannot
subsist superactually but, analogously to certain
states or sensations, are restricted in their existence
to the mere actual experience. The role of superactual responses is plainly enormous in our life. The
most important and fundamental responses are all
capable of subsisting in a superactual way, whether it
is deep sorrow over the loss of a beloved person, love
or veneration for someone, our gratitude toward
another, or above all our faith in and our love of
God. What would be the life of a man if it consisted
merely in experiences which live only so long as they
occupy more or less the center of our momentary

consciousness, if the inevitable rhythm of one replacing another were to extend to all our experiences, that is to say, to our entire inner life, excepting the memory of our experiences and mere capacities, abilities or active potentialities? There would be no place for any continuity, no room for all the plenitude and depth of man.[19]

Von Hildebrand thinks that virtues are superactual responses and commitments (in the sense explained above) of the will and the heart. His discussion of various virtues is in many ways unique because of the central role that the concept of value-response plays in his moral philosophy. As can be seen from the following passages on reverence, goodness, and humility, the virtues he discusses are all elements in the way in which the human person ought to relate to the world of values.

Reverence is the mother of all virtues and in fact of all religion. It is the foundation and the beginning because it enables our spirit to possess real knowledge, and primarily the knowledge of values. It is that fundamental attitude toward being in which one gives all being the opportunity to unfold itself in its specific nature, in which one neither behaves as its master, nor acts toward it in a spirit of familiar conviviality.

. . . In this right and appropriate attitude toward being as such, this affirmation free from obtrusiveness, this silent, contemplative disposition toward being as being, the world begins to disclose itself in its entire depth, differentiation, and plenitude of value. . . . Reverence is thus the foundation of all perception and sense of values. But it is also an indispensable element of every response to value; or, in other words, it is a fundamental component of a true relationship with the world of values. It represents the proper answer to the majesty of values, to the "message" they convey to us of God, of the absolute, the infinitely superior. Only the person who possesses reverence is capable of real enthusiasm, of joy insofar as it is motivated by values, true love, and obedience. The man who lacks reverence is blind to values and incapable of submission to them.[20]

Goodness is the very heart of the whole reign of moral values. It is by no accident that the term "good" means moral value as such, and also the specific moral quality of goodness. Among the different moral values there is none which embodies more completely the entire reign of moral values than goodness; in it we find the purest and most typical expression of the general character of moral goodness as such. It is in the center of all morality, and at the same time, its most sublime fruit . . . not a fruit among others, such as meekness, patience, generosity, but the fruit of fruits, i.e. that in which culminates all morality in a specific way; it is the queen of all virtues.

What is goodness? What do we mean when we say that a man irradiates goodness? We say this of a man when he is disposed to help, when he is kindly, just, when he is ready to make sacrifices for others, when he pardons wrongs done him, when he is generous, when he is full of compassion. All these qualities are specific forms and manifestations of love. This indicates the close connection which exists between love and goodness. Love is, as it were, flowing goodness, and goodness is the breath of love.[21]

... [It is] important to understand that goodness, although it is tender and meek, possesses at the same time the greatest strength. Faced with its irresistible power, with its superior security and freedom, the force of the superman is only miserable weakness and childish pretence. One should not mistake goodness for weak surrender, a surrender without resistance. The truly good man can be immovable when one tries to divert him from the right path, and when the salvation of his neighbor calls imperatively for sternness. He unshakably resists every seduction and temptation.

One should be aware of confusing goodness with good-nature. The good-natured man is harmless and is an appeaser; because of a certain lassitude and inertia of his nature, he lets himself be badly treated without noticing it. His amiable attitude has its source in a completely unconscious tendency of his nature. Goodness, on the contrary, flows from a conscious response of love; it is "ardent awakedness" and never "harmless lassitude." It is the most intensive moral life, and not inertia and dullness; it is strength and not weakness. The good man does not allow himself to be made use of because he lacks the strength to resist, but he serves freely and humbles himself willingly.[22]

Humility involves the full knowledge of our status as creatures, a clear consciousness of having received everything we have from God. . . . Thus, it has been said justly: "Humility is Truth." . . .

True knowledge of our status as creatures, however, implies a confrontation of the creature with its creator: it is not possible except in reference to a personal God. For awareness of our creaturely status is more than a mere awareness of our debility and limitation. It amounts to experiencing not only our relative imperfection and the restrictions to which we are subject, but the infinite distance between us and absolute Being; it requires a full understanding of the fact that we have received "all that we have and are"—except sin—from God . . . that He is That Which is, whereas we are "as though we *were not.*"

Furthermore, humility also implies blissful *assent* to this our creatureliness and "non-being." What it demands is not a reluctant or resigned admission of our nothingness: it is, primarily, a joyous response to the infinite glory of God. . . . The humble man does not want to be anything "on his own resources"; he is free from all ambition to be something by his own power, and to have to recognize no master over himself. He *wills* to receive everything from God alone. The glory of God makes him happy; he is thus so centered in his love of adoration for God that the idea of "being something by his own force"—aside from its unreality—would not tempt him at all; nor does the concern about "keeping his sovereignty intact" carry the slightest meaning to him. Such an attitude, however, is only possible in reference to a personal God, moreover, as Pascal says, "not to the God of the philosophers, but to the God of Abraham, Isaac and Jacob"; above all, to the living God Who approaches and addresses us in the Person of Jesus Christ, His only-begotten Son.[23]

. . . There are those who, while they recognize the glory of God as well as the importance of man and the call addressed to him in general, believe, in false humility, that the call is meant for all others but not for their own person. They deem their own person too wretched to dare assume that they may refer the divine call to themselves. They would hide in a corner and play the part of mere onlookers. The sight of their wretchedness impels them to exclude themselves from the great dialogue between God and man. This ostensible "excess" of humility, for all the diffidence it involves, is not free of an element of pride. For here, once more, man presumes to decide himself where he stands, instead of leaving that decision to God. Yet, this is precisely the test of true humility, that one no longer presumes to judge whether or not one is too miserable to be included in the call to sanctity but simply answers the merciful love of God by sinking down in adoration. The question whether I feel "worthy" to be called is beside the point; that God *has* called me is the one thing that matters. . . .

. . . [T]o the core of humility belongs a gesture of holy audacity. As faith, hope, and charity cannot be without an element of boldness, so also does true humility demand it. Our jubilant assent to our own insignificance, our heroic abandonment of all self-glorification, the relinquishment of self in following Christ—all this is incompatible with tepid mediocrity and cautious smugness. Humility is the opposite, not only of all *malicious* pride but of all forms of self-centered mediocrity. . . . Whereas the virtue of modesty, operating on the level of earthly relationships, is linked to an attitude of quiet reserve or even resignation in which there is no place for boldness, humility implies a heavenward aspiration that carries with it a breath of greatness and holy audacity. The total relinquishment of self, the blissful dying away of the ego—this means an ultimate jubilant freedom; an unthwarted subsistence in truth.[24]

Beauty and Utilitarianism

Von Hildebrand's sensitivity to the world of values and his insight into the importance of this world for the happiness of the human person led him to be very critical of the "utilitarian mentality" which looks upon many values as useless and empty luxuries.

For the utilitarian mentality the *bonum utile* becomes the one exclusive measure of judging things. What is not useful is declared useless, with no right to existence. It is considered a waste of time, something futile and utterly lacking in seriousness. Goods endowed with a high value, such as the liturgical praise of God, all bonds of love with other persons, all beauty, the whole sphere of art, philosophy; in short, all the things which are not practically indispensable, are classed together with the superfluous and marked

as useless. The whole sphere of the genuine *frui*—
the enjoyment of high goods endowed with values
which bestow a true and noble happiness on us—is
put in one category together with luxuries and those
things which are considered a waste of time. By force
of a wrong exclusive alternative the sphere of the elementary goods (enlarged more or less arbitrarily)
and all that serves their attainment are considered
serious, dignified, and worthwhile; while everything
else is considered worthless and futile, or merely
romantic. A gray and neutral reasonability is exalted;
a pedestrian attitude prevails wherein the sublimity
of values fades and the fruition of great and noble
goods is silently ignored.[25]

In his essay, Beauty in the Light of the Redemption,
*von Hildebrand defends the importance of beauty against
what might be called a kind of Christian utilitarianism
which argues that beauty "belongs to the sphere of luxury,
to that part of life which, in the light of Christ, cannot lay
claim to belong to the serious aspect of life," and that an
earnest Christian "must concentrate upon great economic,
political, and social problems." He argues, first, that this
way of thinking is not in line with the spirit of the Gospel.*

I respond: this utilitarianism is by no means the spirit of the Gospel. Certainly, in the light of our eternal
salvation, the *unum necessarium* (the one thing necessary), beauty of form is secondary, but this is equally
true of economic and social problems. . . .

An estimate of all things from the viewpoint of
their practical and absolute necessity or a restriction

of them to that which is absolutely necessary—a spirit that is legitimately master of the technical sciences—is to be found neither in God's creation nor in the Revelation of Christ. In these latter, on the contrary, the principle of superabundance rules. . . .

The first miracle of Christ at the wedding feast of Cana reveals to us in a glorious manner the superabundance of divine love, which shows no restriction to that which is necessary. The wine was not at all indispensable for the wedding feast. It was not even entirely wanting, but there was simply lacking a sufficiency. Certainly the primary meaning of this miracle was the manifestation of Christ's divinity. Yet, does not the fact that the content of the miracle has reference only to heightening the resplendence of the feast imply a radical renunciation of all forms of utilitarianism? . . .

No, indispensability of a thing is one point of view, the value of a thing another. The fact that beauty of form is not indispensable does not affect its value and its seriousness.[26]

Second, von Hildebrand points out that beauty is the foundation of love and therefore plays a crucial role in drawing us towards all that is good and holy.

[It] naturally has a conspicuous function in the life of the Christian, for this beauty is the foundation of love. The divine beauty of Jesus, the beauty of the Saint of all saints, inflames our heart. It shone resplendent on the apostles on Mount Tabor; the beauty of His divine mercy melted the heart of Mary

Magdalene. The irresistible divine beauty of Jesus
not only moves our will, but it attracts our heart. As
St. Augustine says, "We are attracted not only by the
will but also by delight."

The great Lacordaire says that virtues become
irresistibly victorious and constrain us to love only
when, as in every saint, they are manifested in their
beauty, when their inner nobility is revealed in their
beauty. This beauty is a radiation of the inner preciousness as well as of the qualitative values with
which this being is endowed.[27]

But perhaps the most profound and original contribution
von Hildebrand makes in this context is to point out that
there is a certain type of beauty ("beauty of form") which
is not just a reflection of the being to which it belongs, but
contains something much more. The beauty of a painting,
for instance, is not just a reflection of the nature of paint
and canvas, but somehow mediates to us a higher world.
Far from distracting us from the essential, therefore, such
beauty lifts us above ourselves and draws us closer to God,
the source of all beauty.

[T]here is a special message of God, a specific reflection of God's infinite beauty, contained in a glorious
landscape, such as the one seen from the Parthenon
in Athens or from the Giannicolo in Rome; in the
sublimity of a church such as San Marco in Venice,
and in the transfigured music of Beethoven's Ninth
Symphony or in one of his late quartets. This beauty
speaks of a world above; it is a ray of the Father of all

Lights; it elevates our spirit and fills our heart with a longing for this higher world.[28] . . .

. . . It is a great mystery that God has entrusted to visible and audible objects the ability to place before us sublime, spiritual qualities: a beauty which, in its quality, reflects God's world and which speaks of this higher transfigured world. The function of the senses and of the visible and audible contents in this experience is of a modest, humble kind: they are a pedestal, a mirror for something much higher. . . .

This is also brought out distinctly in the answer we give to beauty of form. . . . Our heart is filled with a desire for loftier regions about which this beauty speaks, and it looks upward with longing.

In order to behold this beauty, we need not know God, much less think of Him; once we fully grasp this beauty it leads us to God, for objectively there is a reflection of Him in these things and not merely in the manner in which all that exists reflects God. Here in things of a relatively low ontological rank something *appears* which surpasses by far their rank and heralds God in a more intimate way in its own quality. Only when we have understood this quasi-sacramental function of the visible and audible, this mystery that God has entrusted to it, can we do justice to the function of this beauty in the life of the redeemed.

It is not true that this beauty distracts us from God and is specifically mundane. On the contrary, it contains a summons; in it there dwells a call to us to lift up our hearts; it awakens reverence in us; it elevates us above that which is base; it fills our hearts with a longing for the eternal beauty of God.[29]

The Heart

As mentioned in the introduction, von Hildebrand greatly deepens and enriches our philosophical understanding of the human person by restoring the heart, i.e. the center of our affective life, to its rightful place in our thinking about the human person. He does this by showing that emotions, such as joy or gratitude, are not just blind passions to be controlled by the intellect and will, but that they are personal responses, which, in their own way, are just as "spiritual" as intellectual and volitional responses, in the sense of being meaningfully related to and motivated by their object. The importance of recognizing the role of the heart in our philosophical conception of the human person becomes apparent when we realize how truly central it is. In one place von Hildebrand writes, "It is in the affective sphere, in the heart, that the treasures of man's most individual life are stored. It is in the heart that the secret of a person is found. . . ."[30] The following passage develops the same thought at greater length.

In order to understand the nature of the heart, we must realize that in many respects the heart is more the real self of the person than his intellect or will.

In the moral sphere it is the will which has the character of a last, valid word. Here the voice of our free spiritual center counts above all.

We find the true self primarily in the will. In many other domains, however, it is the *heart* which is the most intimate part of the person, the core, the real self, rather than the will or the intellect. This is so in the realm of human love: conjugal love, friendship, filial love, parental love. The heart is here not only the true self because love is essentially a voice of the heart; it is also the true self insofar as love aims at the heart of the beloved in a specific way. The lover wants to pour his love into the heart of the beloved, he wants to affect his heart, to fill it with happiness; and only then will he feel that he has really reached the beloved, his very self.

Furthermore, when we love a person and long for a return of our love, it is the heart of the other person which we want to call ours. As long as he only willed to love us and merely conformed his will to our wishes, we should never believe that we really possess his true self. Much as the conformity of his will to our expectations, his friendly looks, and the attentions dictated by his will may touch us from a moral point of view, we would yet feel that he escapes us, that his true self is not ours. As long as we feel that the benefits he bestows on us, his considerations and his sacrifices, are dictated only by a good and generous will, we know that we do not really possess the beloved, because we do not possess his heart.[31]

One might object that the heart cannot represent the "real self" of the person because it is not free. Affective responses such as joy typically "well up" in us whether we will them to or not. Here is von Hildebrand's deep response to this difficulty.

It is indeed a surprising fact that something which arises spontaneously and as a gift in the soul should be a manifestation of a person's true self to a higher degree than that which is an utterance of his free spiritual center. The situation we encounter in the realm of morality seems more intelligible. The word of the person, the valid ultimate word in which his self lives more than in anything else, is the "yes" or "no" of his will. His free intention, what he actualizes with his free spiritual center, is what is really himself. . . .

To begin with, we must realize that the question of whether or not an experience is within the range of our freedom cannot simply be used as a measure to determine the rank of an experience. Freedom is indeed an essential mark of the person as an image of God. But what may also mark the specific high rank of a thing is the fact that it can be granted to us only as a gift. . . .

Typical of man's createdness is the existence of a depth dimension of his soul which does not fall under his mastery as do his volitional acts. Man is greater and deeper than the range of things he can control with his free will; his being reaches into mysterious depths which go far beyond what he can engender or create. Nothing expresses this fact more adequately perhaps than the truth that God is nearer to us than we are to ourselves. And this applies not only to the supernatural level, but also analogously to the natural sphere.

These affections of the higher level, then, [such as "deep contrition, the gift of tears, a deep and ardent love, 'being moved' on hearing sublime music or when witnessing an act of superabundant charity] are truly gifts"—natural gifts of God which man cannot give himself by his own power. Coming as they do from the very depth of his person, they are in a specific way voices of his true self, voices of his full personal being.

It now becomes more intelligible why in certain domains the heart is more the true self than the will. Yet we must add that the full voice of the heart demands the cooperation of the free spiritual center of the person. . . .

. . . [A]ffective experiences which are gifts from above become fully ours, that is to say, they become ultimately valid expressions of our entire personality only when they are sanctioned by our free spiritual center. Our deep love for another person is a gift from above—something we cannot give to ourselves; yet only when we join this love with the "yes" of our free spiritual center does it have the character of a full self-donation. We not only endorse this love, but by this freely spoken "yes" we make it the full and express word of our own. This "yes" of our free center can be spoken only if a high affective experience is granted us. It presupposes the presence of a voice of our heart which is a gift from above.[32]

In the next passage, von Hildebrand sheds further light on the important and distinct role of the heart in the human person.

Here we must again repeat that the heart has a function other than the will, and that God has entrusted the heart to "speak" an irreplaceable word, a word which sometimes differs from that to which the will is called. It would be a disastrous error to overlook this fact and to think that the heart and will must always speak the same word. To deny that God has entrusted the heart to speak a word of its own leads to the conviction that the silencing of the heart is a religious ideal.

The call of God directed to our will has to be obeyed, whatever our heart may feel, or however it may object. But this does not at all imply that our heart should conform itself to the will in the sense that it should speak the same word as the will speaks.

Abraham, after hearing God's command that he sacrifice his son Isaac, had to say "yes" with his will. But his heart had to bleed and respond with the greatest sorrow. His obedience to the commandment would not have been more perfect had his heart responded with joy. On the contrary, it would have been a monstrous attitude. According to the will of God, the sacrifice of his son called for a response of Abraham's heart, namely, that of deepest sorrow. But notwithstanding the deep reluctance of his heart, Abraham was obliged to accept this terrible cross and to conform his will to God's commandment. . . .

If we ask, for instance, what the attitude pleasing to God is when a beloved person dies, our answer is that with our free spiritual center we should speak our *fiat*; we should accept the terrible cross imposed on us. This acceptation is an act of will. But it is meant as a cross by God and this implies that our heart bleeds. The cross would have no place in our life if our heart conformed to God's will in the sense that everything that God permits could only gladden our heart. The great and deep mission of the cross would be frustrated if holiness implied that as soon as something sad happens, and thus is at least *permitted* by God, the heart should no longer worry about it. And not only the role of the cross, but the fully personal character of man, would be frustrated. Man is not simply an instrument, he is a person to whom God addresses himself, whom God treats as a person, since it depends upon man's free will, his free decision, whether or not he will attain his eternal welfare. God also wants man to have his own individual life, to take positions with his heart, to direct himself to God with petition prayers for legitimate high goods in his life. . . .

. . . Man would be a mere mask, he would no longer have his specific individual life; none of the gifts of God entrusted to him during his life would really reach him; he would no longer have a real history, he would not possess a unique unrepeatable existence, if his heart did not give responses to all real goods—responses of gratitude, of longing, of hope, of love.

Man could no longer live a full human life if his heart spoke the same fiat that his will speaks in all those cases where the endangering of a good endowed with a high value, or the loss of it, calls for a specific response of our heart. We emphasize here the sameness of the fiat, because the heart also speaks a certain fiat as opposed to any murmuring. The heart also submits to God's will in throwing itself into the loving arms of God, but it does not for that reason cease to suffer. We need only think of the words of our Lord in Gethsemane, *Pater mi, si possibile est, transeat a me calix iste,* "Father, if it is possible, remove this chalice from me.[33]

In the moral life, too, especially the Christian moral life, we find that the heart plays a central role.

Whereas rectitude and justice are the core of natural morality, in Christian morality the specific center is the goodness of charity. . . .

In this luminous and victorious goodness, the voice of the heart plays a predominant role. If we compare the glorious martyrdom of St. Stephen as told in the Acts of the Apostles with the noble death of Socrates as described in Plato's *Phaedo*, we cannot but grasp the completely new role played by the heart in the followers of Christ. In the martyrdom of St. Stephen, there is a noble spirituality that involves the superabundance of the heart.

Indeed, a transfigured affectivity permeates Christian morality.[34]

Responses of the heart are, as we have seen, not in our immediate control. In some ways, especially when dealing with intense emotions, we feel uncomfortably "out of control" and "carried away." It is crucial, in this respect, to distinguish between two very different kinds of "being out of control," only one of which is salutary, and compatible with our personal dignity and freedom.

[T]here are two ways of being "out of our minds," which are radically opposed to each other, although they are both antithetical to the normal state which is characterized by the fact that we feel solid ground under our feet, that our reason clearly oversees the situation, and that our will chooses with ease.

The low way of "being out of our mind" . . . is characterized by irrationality. It implies a blurring of our reason which precludes its most modest use. Not only is our reason confused, but it is also throttled. Through the brutal dynamism of this state, both reason and the free spiritual center of the person are engulfed. Our free spiritual center is overpowered and one is dragged into a brutal biological dynamism. Needless to say, this dynamism is non-spiritual.

In the higher way of "being out of our mind," that is, being in ecstasy, or in every experience of being "possessed" by something greater than we are, we find the very opposite of the passionate state. When someone is moved by a good endowed with a high value to such an extent that he is elevated above the normal rhythm of his life, he also "loses," as it were, the solid ground under his feet. He abandons the comfortable situation in which his reason sovereignly oversees everything and in which his will is able to calculate coolly what he should decide.

But this does not result from a blurring of one's reason but, on the contrary, from its extraordinary elevation by an intuitive awareness which, far from being irrational, has rather a suprarational and luminous character. So far from being antirational is this higher way that instead of darkening our reason it fills it with a great light. . . .

And far from including any tendency to dethrone our free spiritual center, far from trying forcibly to

overpower our reason and will, an ecstasy calls for a
sanction by our free center; it makes an appeal for
this sanction. This "ecstasy" in the largest sense of
the word is fundamentally opposed to any enslave-
ment, to any overruling of our freedom. It is a gift
which implies an elevation to a higher freedom in
which our heart (and not only our will) responds in
the way in which it should respond. It is a liberation
from the fetters holding us down.[35]

*Von Hildebrand points to and rejects the widespread ten-
dency, even among Christians, to equate strong emotions
with irrationality or to identify emotional neutrality with
objectivity. He shows that on the contrary true objectivity
frequently involves the heart; certain things and situations
in human life "call for" an emotional response on our part.
In such cases, failure to "be emotional" is evidence of hard-
heartedness or insensibility, not exemplary objectivity.*

[A]n ethos of prosaic neutrality, of cool distance, free
from every kind of enthusiasm and ardor, an ethos
which is anti-affective, in which every fullness of the
heart is immediately interpreted as exaggerated and
exalted—is this ethos required by objectivity in our
sense of the term?

[Underlying this mistaken view is] a misunder-
standing of the spiritual and meaningful character of
the person's affective responses to value. Because one
disregards the nature of values, one also fails to realize that they call for an affective response on the part
of the person. One fails to grasp that the adequate
response to a sublime work of art is enthusiasm and

emotion, and not a mere acknowledgement of its value. One overlooks the fact that an heroic moral attitude of our neighbor, an act of love toward his enemies, calls for veneration and enthusiasm on our part and not just for a cool, appreciative confirmation. . . .

It is true that, in contradistinction to intellectual attitudes, affective responses relate to the vital sphere, and that when they reach a certain intensity they involve also the corporeal sphere. We can cite, for instance, experiences such as crying from emotion and all other accompanying organ sensations that follow affective attitudes.

However, these experiences are simply accompanying manifestations of these attitudes and do not constitute the attitudes themselves. They in no way change the specifically spiritual character of these attitudes as such. Are we entitled to call something *unspiritual* because it touches the person to such a depth that it also affects other spheres? The meaningful, rational nature of these spiritual, affective attitudes does not consist in disowning their affective character and evincing the distance and coolness of intellectual probing. Rather, their spiritual, rational nature consists in the fact that they address themselves meaningfully to an object in a specifically affective manner, with full ardor. It further consists in the fact that they are consciously and meaningfully related to an object, and that this connection is no mere link of efficient causality. Moreover, their spiritual character manifests itself in the fact that they can be freely sanctioned by the person.[36]

The second part of von Hildebrand's great work, The Heart, *consists of an extended and beautiful reflection on the mystery of the Sacred Heart and what it reveals about the affectivity of Jesus, who is the self-revelation of God. The first passage I have selected is a meditation on the suffering of the Sacred Heart.*

If the "Eli, Eli, lama sabachtani" is the deepest descent into the unfathomable abyss of suffering, the destitution of the soul, the *Sitio*, "I thirst," is the deepest descent into another dimension, that of human frailty, of man's dependence upon his body. It is an ineffable expression of the divine humility, of the one "who emptied himself taking the nature of a slave."

In this supreme moment we are reaching in the role assumed by the body a culmination of the tension of the mystery of the Incarnation. The Lord who is never recorded as mentioning any bodily distress expresses his "thirst" in this supreme moment. His fatigue is mentioned only by the evangelist in the Gospel of the Samaritan woman, and his hunger in the Gospel of the temptations. But here a descent into human helplessness takes place to the point of calling on the "mercy" of his executioners. Mystery of divine humility! The Lord who always gives, who changes water into wine, who feeds the five thousand with five loaves of bread, who gives sight to the blind, who wakes Lazarus from death, this Lord speaks of his thirst here, in the supreme moment of his sacrifice. In this word, revelation is even less the theme than in any other word spoken from the

Cross. The fact that it implies an appeal to man makes it the very antithesis of revelation, a pure expression of his suffering, while yet revealing a deep secret of his passion. Moreover, this implicit request is not addressed to his disciples but to the merciless soldiers. Christ's appeal to their mercy makes this cry the most dramatic expression of his suffering and of his destitution, the deprivation of all his divine might and glory.[37]

The Sacred Heart reveals not only God's deep love for us, but also His desire to be loved by us in return.

The unveiling of his Sacred Heart continues after the resurrection. In the apparition to Mary Magdalene, a glance is granted to us into the Sacred Heart of the gloriously risen Christ. He reveals himself to Mary Magdalene with the one word, "Maria." The very uttering of her name includes in this situation an unveiling of his Heart. A tender love and a glorious joy are present in this making himself known as Jesus. Ineffable intimacy and glory of this situation! On the one hand, the longing of Mary Magdalene, her despair over the Lord's death, her loving desire to find at least his body; and on the other hand, the response of Jesus in revealing himself to her even before the apostles. In disclosing his identity as the risen Christ by the sound of his voice, and by calling her by her name, Jesus unveiled his Sacred Heart.

. . . "Simon son of John, dost thou love me more than these do?" These words, repeated three times by the risen Lord, are spoken by the God-Man Christ, the Redeemer, the one who will come again "to judge the living and the dead."

The appeal to the love of Peter reveals the unfathomable mystery that Christ seeks our love, that he wants not only to be obeyed but also to be loved. It reveals this sublime tenderness, a revelation which acquires a specific import through the fact that it is repeated three times and is one of the last words of Christ. It is related at the end of St. John's Gospel; it is only after all the apparitions of the risen Lord. If the words *mihi est data omnis potestas in coelo et in terra*, "all power in heaven and on earth has been given to me," spoken immediately before the Ascension, are the ultimate revelation of Christ's divinity, the manifestation of his absolute Lordship, these words are the last effusion of his Sacred Heart. They breathe an ineffable meekness and gloriously tender love. And in the divine *Pasce oves meas*, "Feed my sheep," we discern the trembling love for all those who have followed him, for all those who will ever follow him.[38]

Love and Community

It is deeply characteristic of the human person to be made for communion with other human persons. Von Hildebrand has thought and written much about this. In the next passage he explains how important true communion is to the full flowering of human life, and how it is impossible to achieve fully except through God.

An isolated man, one who has not become conscious of the ultimate objective link binding him to all other men before God, is an unawakened, immature, even a mutilated man. That liberal conception which considers the "solitary" man as the great, profound human being is the logical outcome of the understanding of communion as something peripheral in its nature. Of course, a true personality is, in one sense, solitary among average men, because this personality is alone in his knowledge of that deep communion to which average men have not awakened; he is not satisfied with the superficialities of mere interest or pleasure and seeks a profounder link. . . . But a true personality is never solitary in the sense of being isolated from others in the depths, in the sense of indifference or hostility; he is not unalive to that ultimate, triumphant unity with his brother, whom he sees in the place where each man in truth stands before God, whether he is aware of it or not. The fathers of the desert and the hermits lived entirely in that spirit of true communion, unlike their pagan contemporaries inhabiting crowded cities, surrounded by other men and bound to them by peripheral ties. The true measure of the depth of a man will much rather be found in whether or not he is awakened to that spirit of true communion, in whether or not there has been a breaking-down of the inner walls of self-assertion, in the defenses of the sphere of his ego.

The shutting up of oneself in this inner fortress of isolation, which exists secretly even in the most jovial joiner of clubs, is proof of narrowness, limitation, even stupidity. For it presupposes a certain egocentric attitude toward the world and God. The man who has been melted by the sun of values, and above all the man who has been wounded by the love of Christ, is also lovingly open to every man and has entered into the objective unity of all. Yes, this ultimate true spirit of communion, the universal disposition to love, and the life in the ultimate loving "We," is only possible as a fruit of the ultimate "I-thou-communion" with Christ, through which we are transfigured into Christ. Every attempt to achieve this "We" without Christ leads to a superficially anchored pseudo-communion. It suffices to recall, for instance, the humanitarian idea. Every attempt to achieve a "We" which does not pass through the "thou" of the God-man, fails to achieve the full conquest of egocentricity; on the contrary, it leads to mass-egoism, which is perhaps even lower than the egoism of the individual, in its pretension to be an ultimate liberation from the imprisonment of self.[39]

We have seen above the importance of value and value-response for the full flowering of the human person. That they are also crucial for interpersonal communion is shown in the following passage, on the virtus unitiva *of values.*

A unifying power inheres deeply in values themselves, they possess a *virtus unitiva* which is of the essence of value. The opposite also holds: a divisive power inheres in all disvalues, a power that deeply isolates the person who gives himself to them. . . .

The human person has an "outer" and an "inner" side. When he is closed off, he touches the other only with his "outer side" and also touches the other from the outside. Something completely new happens as soon as man opens himself, lets his inner side appear and lets it touch the other person. Every experience of being deeply moved by value means such a breakthrough of the inner side, a self-opening of the person towards all others, that are now grasped from within and viewed in their metaphysical situation.

The opening-up of a man, who is touched by a ray of the world of value and beauty, is simultaneously an opening-up in the direction of other persons. While the crust of indifference, of egoism, and of pride, which forms on the outside of the person and closes him off from the other, melts under the influence of being moved by the world of values, a union with all other persons constitutes itself simultaneously. The breakthrough of the depth of the person who is taken by the embracing rays of the realm of values . . . is simultaneously a falling away of the separating barriers between persons.

. . . The person who is truly caught by the "breath" of values and thereby "opened up", finds himself in a loving fundamental attitude, gentle and free, and not only open to others, but rather drawing them all into his love.

Certainly, the *peripheral* bond with other persons, such as a bond of mere sociability, is ruptured by such a deep experience. The others can even be a hindrance when we are truly gripped by a real value. We then naturally seek solitude, but only because that kind of social bond keeps us in the peripheral.

The solitude one looks for does not imply a real separation from the others, but is rather only a way to
find the others in a deeper way. One has to free oneself from peripheral bonds, to be bound to other persons in the depths.[40]

*Von Hildebrand recognized that part of the attraction of
National Socialism lay in the powerful (if delusive) sense
of community it gave its adherents. It seemed to overcome
the problems of petty and isolating individualism, by
drawing people up into a force and purpose greater than
themselves. But it did so at the expense of the individual
person, and therefore, inescapably, at the expense of any
true communal life. Here is a particularly representative
passage, taken from an article published by von
Hildebrand in the journal he founded in Vienna to do bat-
tle with the twin ideologies of German National Socialism
(Nazism) and Communism.*

Though we are benefited deeply by the moral help of
community, as when we gain better insight into certain things by living in the spiritual space of a community, or when something becomes clear to us here
that would be more difficult for us to grasp alone, we
must not confuse these benefits with the illegitimate
loss of all critical spirit or with "being thrown into a
depersonalized mass." The community, which in an
ordered, meaningful way "unifies" human beings as
spiritual persons, implies great support and help for
the individual person in the forming of resolutions,
in the readiness to act heroically, in the adherence to
convictions. This support by the community does

not undermine the individual's integrity and rob him of his responsibility; it does not have the function of replacing legitimate conviction; rather, it creates a spiritual space which facilitates the ability to gain insight because this space is itself shaped and formed by these ideas; it helps one to draw the consequences from these insights. . . .

But the desire for the legitimate aid to and enhancement of our subjectivity through genuine community, the need to be embedded in a solidarity that does not stem from our arbitrary will, can stray terribly when it seeks fulfillment in a depersonalized mass. The fleeting, sensational intoxication of the mass situation, which is quickly followed by disillusionment . . . is a world apart from the noble elevation that derives from living in genuine community. Here too, as with most contemporary aberrations, we encounter anti-personalism as a primary root of all evil. We must once and for all stop elevating community at the expense of the individual. We must grasp that community cannot be pitted against the person. The individual person and community are ordered to one another in such a way that we will never be able to understand the true nature of community if we do not clearly acknowledge man as a spiritual person made in the image of God, and, on the other hand, that we will never do justice to the nature of the person and the fullness of his being if we do not fully understand the nature of community. Modern anti-personalism as we encounter it in Bolshevism and National Socialism does not represent a victory over liberal individualism but its ultimate and most radical consequence. Only the rehabilitation of man as a spiritual person, as a being with an immortal soul destined to eternal community with God, can save us from being dissolved into a depersonalized mass and lead us to real community.[41]

Man and Woman

Von Hildebrand has written much and profoundly on the nature of conjugal love, marriage, and sexuality. Below are a few examples of the gems to be found in these works. The first passage distinguishes between the sympathetic way in which love interprets the faults of the beloved and the tendency to idealize someone, which is often confused with it.

Love is always assuming what is best in the other. So long as there is no reason for reckoning with the presence of a fault, love entertains the more favorable . . . opinion toward all that is doubtful. When love encounters a fault in the other, it is like meeting disloyalty or infidelity to what is truest in his nature (it is never accepted on a par with his positive qualities). . . .

One should not confuse this credit of love, however, with the inclination to idealize, which is typical of day-dreamers. Generosity which is typical of love presupposes the existence of a corresponding value which justifies and gives it meaning. But where there are only dreams, the central thing is a need to experience delight and to have contact with admirable and extraordinary people. Pleasure of this sort is so strongly desired that one commits himself to an imaginary ideal. One enjoys dreaming. The person one idealizes is more an occasion for dreaming than a meaningful subject to be taken seriously in himself. One imagines that everything about the other is splendid and grand, although one has had no opportunity to know him well enough to be so certain. The difference between such an unfounded attitude and the faithful credit of love, to which we have already made reference, is what we shall now consider. . . .

Love's generous credit is intimately bound up with its surrender. The loving person in no way seeks his own gratification. He is oriented completely toward the other. And his trusting conviction is completely for the other's sake, having nothing whatever of self-gratification about it. The dream, however, is always for gratification's sake. It does not have the other person in mind, but rather him who dreams.

This credit has nothing of extravagance about it. It goes hand in hand with the realization that a noble man is also quite frail and weak. Where everything seems to be in order, love reckons with the possibility that there may be imperfections which must be faced as unpleasant but temporary facts, even though it will never be prejudiced by them. The loving credit does not dwell in an ethereal or unreal region. It does not mount Pegasus. Rather it fortifies itself on ground which is altogether real, characterized by holy surroundings.

Nor is the radical difference between loving

credit and dreaming fancy somehow diminished by the fact that one can also be disappointed where love is authentic or that credit can sometimes come to real disappointment itself. It is not the possibility of disappointment that makes the dreamer's fancies to be what they are. They are characterized, rather, by the absence of true love, by the ethereal, unreal, and even deceptive atmosphere in which the life of desire is led. One could say: the lover can be disappointed; the dreamer deceives himself.[42]

Here is a beautiful passage on the indissolubility of marriage, which far from being burdensome or detrimental to genuine conjugal love, is rather the fulfillment of its specific nature.

The indissolubility of marriage has an important retroactive effect on conjugal love. It is considered by many as something oppressive and dispiriting, something which deprives love of its wings and gives it a coercive character. They think that love would vanish with the knowledge that the tie is binding whether love persists or not. But nothing is less true. For the real lover, the consciousness of being indissolubly united with his beloved in Christ, of forming an objectively indissoluble community whose validity is beyond all wavering and all human frailties, is a source of the highest satisfaction. For he wants to be one with his beloved, and he is grateful and happy that this unity can be realized to so great a degree and that it rises above all emotional changes.

Conjugal love implies an intention of *going beyond*

even the giving of self, which is inherent in love as such. It desires an objective self-giving once and for ever, an irrevocable giving which persists independently of all subjective inconstancy. . . .

. . . The true lover experiences the objective validity of his self-bestowal, and the accomplishment of such a transcendent, irrevocable decision, as a specific fulfillment of his love.

Certainly this decision involves a great risk; and when the choice of the spouse happens to be based on an illusion, the indissolubility of marriage may prove a great cross for one or both consorts. But it lies in the nature of conjugal love to be bold, heroic, not to shrink back from taking a risk. *All great things on earth are connected with risk*. Without risk, human life—*in statu viae*—would be deprived of all grandeur and heroism. . . .

Marriage is not a bourgeois affair, a kind of insurance for happiness, providing a way of escape from every eventual cross. Does not every love as such carry with it a great risk of suffering? In attaching our hearts to a person, do we not run the risk of enduring terrible sufferings, through misfortunes that may happen to our beloved or separation from her when she dies? Should we then abstain from love in order to prevent the possibility of great sorrow?

He whose life is dominated by the intention of avoiding any possible cross excludes everything that gives human life grandeur and depth. He will never know real abandon—never know real, deep happiness. Remaining in a mediocre self-centeredness, he will never be able to do anything without a certain reserve; he will always provide for a possibility of retreat.[43]

When love is misunderstood as a "mere feeling," blinding, unreliable and inconstant, it is easy to understand why one would want to make sure that marriages are built on other, more solid and reasonable grounds. But when love is properly understood it becomes clear that it is the motive par excellence *for marriage.*

Even in Catholic circles we often find the disastrous concept of a *reasonable marriage*. By this is meant a marriage which issues not from so-called *sentiment* but from rational considerations.

This implies a wrong alternative. Obviously, the decision to marry someone should also be a subject of examination by our intellect—but the precise subject of that intellectual examination should be the question of whether the conjugal love (which is here rather contemptuously treated as sentiment) really exists between both persons, whether the prospective spouse is really what she seems to be, whether she is the person whom God destined for me, whether the projected union is something pleasing to God, and whether there is any danger in this union for her eternal welfare or for mine.

But as soon as the intellect turns to matters not relevant to marriage or to matters of secondary importance, or—even worse—makes these considerations in themselves the motive of marriage, it misses completely its proper role, which is to consider and clarify that preexisting love which is the proper motive for marriage. How could we refer to a marriage of this kind as other than *unreasonable?* To be reasonable, an attitude must be in conformity with the nature and meaning of the thing to which it is referred. . . .

A so-called *marriage of reason* (which is decided after a cold calculation that one's financial situation can be improved and certain professional advantages attained, or that both are peaceful and will get on together, or that their ages are well suited)—a marriage where such considerations (rather than conjugal love) constitute the motivation, where there is no longing for an indissoluble community with the beloved, is not only deprived of all beauty and plenitude, but is also something definitely *unreasonable*.[44]

Von Hildebrand was among the first clearly to articulate a distinction, which later found its way into the encyclical Humanae Vitae *and into the Second Vatican Council's pastoral constitution,* Gaudium et spes, *between the unitive and procreative meanings of marriage and sexuality. Here the distinction is used to shed light on the evil of promiscuity.*

He alone can understand the horror of the sin of promiscuity who has grasped the grandeur and sublimity of bodily union as the full realization of conjugal love, and who realizes that besides the primary *end* of procreation, the primary *meaning* of bodily union lies in the fulfillment of conjugal love. . . .

. . . Were procreation not only the end but also the *sole meaning* of this union, it would be incomprehensible, in the last analysis, why an illegitimate union should be sinful when children result from it, and a marriage pure and sublime when it serves only the communion of love in a childless marriage.[45]

Von Hildebrand's deep grasp of the intimate union between body and soul, especially in the sexual sphere, enables him to see that sex is not a mere biological or bodily phenomenon, and that it can never be taken lightly, because it necessarily and deeply involves the persons engaged in it.

Sex . . . is *essentially* deep. Every manifestation of sex produces an effect which transcends the physical sphere and . . . involves the soul deeply in its passion. . . .

And, as a result, it is characteristic of sex that in virtue of its very significance and nature it tends to become incorporated with experiences of a higher order, purely psychological and spiritual. Nothing in the domain of sex is so self-contained as the other bodily experiences, e.g., eating and drinking. The unique profundity of sex in the physical sphere is sufficiently shown by the simple fact that a man's attitude towards it is of incomparably greater moral significance than his attitude to other bodily appetites. Surrender to sexual desire for its own sake defiles a man in a way that gluttony, for example, can never do. It wounds him to the core of his being, and he becomes in an absolutely different and novel fashion guilty of sin. And even as compared with many other domains of experience which are not physical, sex occupies a central position in the personality. It

represents a factor in human nature which essentially seeks to play a decisive part in a man's life. Sex can
indeed keep silence, but when it speaks it is no mere
obiter dictum, but a voice from the depths, the utterance of something central and of the utmost significance. In and with sex, man, in a special sense, gives
himself.[46]

*The beautiful passage below explains why it is that only
wedded love (and not a mere act of the will) can elevate the
sexual sphere and permeate it in such a way as to become
a genuine expression of self-donation.*

Only wedded love . . . as a special kind of love and as
love in wedlock, is able to transform the act of wedded union from within and make it truly pure. How
then is this transformation effected, and why is this
love alone capable of accomplishing it? Love alone, as
the most fruitful and most intense act, the act which
brings the entire spirit into operation, possesses the
requisite power to transform thoroughly the entire
qualitative texture of an experience. The will, the
informing power in the sphere of conduct, can, as it
were, grasp our emotional experiences only from the
outside. It can—indeed, for this its assent is suffi-
cient—*liberate* the person from an experience; can, for
instance, render his envy up to a certain point harmless, can "behead" it, or immure it within the person;
but it cannot destroy it, as love destroys it. By his will
the person can, so to speak, overleap his emotional
life with a magnificent gesture, but he cannot change
its quality. Hence the will by itself can never effect an

organic union between sex on the one hand and the heart and mind on the other. Whatever the aim the will sets before itself, so long as the act of marriage is motivated by the will alone, it remains a foreign body within the life of the spirit, and though possibly free from sin, it remains, nevertheless, something without organic connection with the life of the person, its brutal aggressor, something which simply co-exists with the heart and the mind and therefore retains a certain animality. As we have already seen, the mere relation to an end can never impart an inner significance to the act of marriage as an experience, still less ennoble it. Love, on the other hand, can wholly dissolve any experience and transform the quality of its texture; in more technical language, can strip its *matter* of the old *form* and invest it with a new.[47]

Liturgy, Prayer, and the Transformation in Christ

Transformation in Christ *begins with a beautiful chapter on the readiness to change which every Christian must possess to make true progress in his walk with God. This readiness to change, von Hildebrand insists, must be total.*

A strong desire must fill us to become different beings, to mortify our old selves and re-arise as new men in Christ. This desire, this readiness to "decrease" so that "He may grow in us," is the first elementary precondition for the transformation in Christ. . . . Our surrender to Christ implies a readiness to let Him fully transform us, without setting any limit to the modification of our nature under His influence.[48]

There are many religious Catholics whose readiness to change is merely a conditional one. They exert themselves to keep the commandments and to get rid of such qualities as they have recognized to be sinful. But they lack the will and the readiness to become new men all in all, to break with all purely natural standards, to view all things in a supernatural light. They prefer to evade the act of *metanoia*: a true "conversion" of the heart. Hence with an undisturbed conscience they cling to all that appears to them legitimate by natural standards. Their conscience permits them to remain entrenched in their self-assertion. For example, they do not feel the obligation of loving their enemies; they let their pride have its way within certain limits; they insist on the right of giving play to their natural reactions in answer to any humiliation. They maintain as self-evident their claim to the world's respect, they dread being looked upon as "fools of Christ"; they accord a certain rôle to human respect, and are anxious to stand justified in the eyes of the world also. They are not ready for a total breach with the world and its standards; they are swayed by certain conventional considerations; nor do they refrain from "letting themselves go" within reasonable limits.[49]

Our transformation in Christ can hardly begin without our first recognizing and repenting of our sins. True penitence also readies the soul for the transformation that needs to take place.

The aspect which is entirely specific to true penitence is that of radical self-surrender. Pride and
obduracy melt away. The natural tendency to self-
assertion which is otherwise so firmly fixed in our
nature—and which makes us reluctant to admit a
wrong we have done, or to ask a person whom we
have wronged to forgive us—is renounced by the
penitent. He surrenders himself in humble charity.
The tight impermeability of his soul towards God
and his fellow creatures disappears. The spasm of
dogmatic obstinacy, forcing him always to "defend
his position," is relaxed. He assumes a state of mind
receptive to the Good in all its forms; he divests himself of all self-preservation to the point of full
defenselessness.

. . . Not only is it indispensable for our transformation into Christ, and our acquisition of that
"fluid" quality which renders us susceptible of such a
transformation, it also imparts to the soul of man a
unique character of beauty. For it is in contrition that
the "new" fundamental attitude of a humble and reverent charity becomes dominant and manifest; that
man abandons the fortress of pride and self-sover-
eignty, and leaves the dreamland of levity and com-
placency, repairing to the place where he faces God
in reality.[50]

Transformation in Christ *includes an illuminating
chapter on the Christian call to be "peacemakers." In it
von Hildebrand describes not only what being a peacemak-
er means, but also what it does not mean. The following
passage stands out as particularly helpful.*

[T]he attitude of rancorous enmity is not the only antithesis to the Christian spirit of forgiveness. Another attitude opposed to it is that of simply ignoring the wrong inflicted upon us, as though nothing had happened. This aberration may result from laziness, from faintness of heart, or from a sickly, mawkish clinging to outward peace. We hold our comfort too dear to "fight it out" with our aggressor; or again, we feel terrified at the thought of any tension or hostility, and fear lest a sharp reaction on our part should exasperate the adversary; or perhaps we yield just out of respect for the abstract idol of peace. This is a kind of behavior far remote from the genuine love of peace or from a genuine spirit of forgiveness. It can never achieve the true harmony of peace, but at best a superficial cloaking of enmity, a mood of false joviality which drags our souls towards the peripheral.

Also, people who behave thus fail to consider the moral damage that their supineness is likely to inflict on others. It is very often necessary to draw a person's attention to the wrong he has done us—in fact, necessary for his own good. To pass over it in silence may easily encourage him in his bad dispositions. But we cannot reproach him to good purpose—that is, without provoking strife—unless we have ourselves attained to that serene attitude cleansed of all impulsive resentment; in other words, unless we have truly forgiven him. . . . [W]hen we have risen above the mood of regarding his awareness or admission of his wrong as a satisfaction to ourselves, then only shall we be able to ponder judiciously and to decide pertinently whether or not it is necessary for us—to remonstrate with him for his good.

All this refers to our disagreements with comparative strangers, persons with whom we are not linked by close bonds of friendship or love. Where such bonds do exist, the case is essentially different. Here it is strictly required by the *logos* of the relationship that our partner shall recognize, and regret the wrong he has done to us. Here we must not quit the "common level" on which we are joined with him, for by so doing we should act against the spirit of the relation that unites us, indeed implicitly disavow our friendship. In this case, the other person has a legitimate claim to the continuance of our being "partners." Most certainly we must forgive him, too; but here we must desire that he recognize and repent of his wrong, not merely for his own good but for the sake of our relationship itself—of the restoration of that intimate union of hearts which essentially demands the clearing up of all misunderstandings and the healing of all disharmonies. For that union of hearts is an objective good which we must guard and cultivate, and which imposes certain obligations on us. True, here as in other cases we must not let the autonomous mechanism of the situation run away with us, and must carefully refrain from repaying an injury in kind. As victims of an aggression *hic et nunc*, we must—under these specific conditions, too— detach ourselves from the situation of the moment, and answer all gestures of irritation, all moral blows with kindness and charity only. Yet, here we can on no account content ourselves with an act of inward forgiveness: at the proper moment, we must in love draw our friend's attention to his wrong, and maintain our desire for his redressing it. However, we cannot do this in the right way before we have truly forgiven him, before all bitterness and irritation on our part have yielded to a purified, unselfish pain. Our admonition should not bear, properly speaking, the note of a reproach. It should rather be in the character of a humble and amicable exposition of our grief, a gentle invitation to our friend to consider the matter in a valid perspective and to collect himself anew, taking his start from that incident on a plane of spiritual earnestness and love. Nevertheless, it remains true that the full harmony implied by the objective *logos* of the relationship is not re-established before our friend has understood and admitted his wrong, until he has asked our pardon for it.

To insist on this condition is not to postpone but to uphold the value of peace. By so acting, we still keep aloof from strife. Our demand that our friend revise his conduct springs from our longing for an unsullied harmony and an enduring intimacy in our relationship with him; that is to say, for peace, perfect and undisturbed.[51]

In Liturgy and Personality, *von Hildebrand discusses the profound effect that regular and attentive participation in the liturgy has on a person. But, characteristically, he first points out that this transformation of the person can be brought about only if it is not the main reason for attending.*

[O]ne of the special reasons for the strength and depth of the transformation of a personality brought about by the Liturgy is that this transformation is not the end in view; and more than this, that the Liturgy is carried out with another intention entirely. For the deepest transformation of personality occurs, not when means for this transformation are deliberately sought, but when it is brought about in an entirely gratuitous manner through an attitude meaningful in itself. This attitude is like that of love which is entirely directed toward its object, a love which in its very essence is a pure response-to-value, which comes into existence only as a response to the value of the beloved, and which would cease to exist as soon as it became a pedagogical means for one's own improvement. From such an attitude emanates a liberating, mellowing, value-disclosing action of incomparable strength and intensity. . . .

The deepest *pedagogical* effect is achieved through that which is not used as a *pedagogical means*: It is achieved through that which, independent of pedagogical action, dispenses it as a *superfluum* or gift of superabundance.[52]

A further feature of the liturgy, intimately connected with the fact that it is the prayer of the universal Church, is that it liberates us from our own narrow perspective and concerns, by drawing us up and into the world of God.

[L]iturgical prayer means emerging from the narrowness of one's own life and rejoining the life of

Christ and the universal sphere of the praying Church. It is an immersion into the world of God. The man who is bound only to God by brief upward glances and good intentions remains fixed in his own life; he moves in a religious atmosphere which corresponds to his own subjective narrowness; he lives on an image of God and Christ which he has formed by himself. . . . [Such men] draw God into *their* lives and see Him through the glasses of their own narrowness; they have lost the sense of true proportion; the air they breathe daily is too much determined by the narrow scope of their particular lives, even though they might be embellished with religion. Such men do not actually emerge from their lives in order to meet God; the fundamental rhythm of their existence is not immersion in God's world and the *magnalia Dei*, nor a participation in the adoring and sacrificing love of Christ; they do not let their lives flow into the life of Christ. This danger cannot be sufficiently stressed![53]

The liturgy, furthermore, in contrast to many other forms of extra-liturgical piety, which seek transformation through some sort of technique of the will, tends to form the person in a thoroughly organic and natural way.

The way to true personality does not lead through the formation of a technique of the will, a decomposition of life into a series of separate, cramped acts, a partitioning of our relations with God into momentary, inorganically linked, quantitatively multiplied little sacrifices, renunciations, appealing glances, and intentions. It does not lead through a petty decomposition of God's commandments into innumerable rules dominating every situation in life from the outside. The way to true personality leads rather through the opening of oneself in the depths, the exposing of oneself to the sun of God; it means being filled with joy by the glory of God, longing to see and to know oneself in His light, in confrontation with Him. This path leads through a love enkindled by the divine beauty of Christ, a love which gives ardor and power to one's will to walk in the ways of the Lord. It implies making room in oneself for the life implanted in us by baptism, giving God the opportunity to speak in us, "watching" before the Lord. It means especially the clear understanding that we are impotent to form Christ in our soul *by our own efforts*, but that the Lord must transform us; that we cannot save our soul by our own power, but only by the power of Christ. It requires prayer for the right thoughts and decisions, prayer for love, grasping the fact that our task is only a free cooperation with grace, letting ourselves be transformed by God. The way to true personality is not through the application of a number of pedagogical rules to our own person, a number of acts which are not accomplished for their own sake but only as a means for a determined aim. What is necessary is the growing into God through value-responses valid in themselves, demanded as such, and not intended as means.

It is along this path that the Liturgy *leads* us.[54]

Endnotes

1. *The New Tower of Babel*, 54–55.
2. *The New Tower of Babel*, 117–21.
3. *The New Tower of Babel*, 133–35.
4. *The New Tower of Babel*, 138–39.
5. *Ethics*, 34–35.
6. *Ethics*, 35–38.
7. *Ethics*, 38–39.
8. *Ethics*, 214–16.
9. *Ethics*, 218.
10. *Ethics*, 210.
11. *Ethics*, 228.
12. *Das Wesen der Liebe* (*The Nature of Love*), Complete English translation forthcoming from St. Augustine's Press (2007).
13. *Liturgy and Personality*, 73–74.
14. *Liturgy and Personality*, 79.
15. *Das Wesen der Liebe* (*The Nature of Love*), Complete English translation forthcoming from St. Augustine's Press.
16. *Ethics*, 316–317.
17. *Transformation in Christ*, 202–3.
18. *Transformation in Christ*, 213–14.
19. *Ethics*, 241–43.

20 *Liturgy and Personality*, 49–51.

21 *The Art of Living*, 41–42.

22 *The Art of Living*, 46–47.

23 *Transformation in Christ*, 127–29.

24 *Transformation in Christ*, 136–38.

25 *Ethics*, 69–70.

26 *The New Tower of Babel*, 161–63.

27 *The New Tower of Babel*, 158–59.

28 *Ethics*, 164.

29 *The New Tower of Babel*, 168–71.

30 *The Heart*, 58.

31 *The Heart*, 67.

32 *The Heart*, 68–71.

33 *The Heart*, 115–17.

34 *The Heart*, 132.

35 *The Heart*, 30–31.

36 *The New Tower of Babel*, 95–101.

37 *The Heart*, 107.

38 *The Heart*, 109–10.

39 *Liturgy and Personality*, 44–46.

40 *Die Metaphysik der Gemeinschaft* (*The Metaphysics of Community*), 99–102.

41 From "Masse und Gemeinschaft" ("Mass and Community"), January 12, 1936, in *Der christliche Ständestaat* (*The Christian Corporative State*).

42 *Man and Woman*, 51–53.

43 *Marriage*, 59–61.

44 *Marriage*, 67–69.

[45] *Marriage*, 30–31.

[46] *In Defense of Purity*, 12–14.

[47] *In Defense of Purity*, 98–99.

[48] *Transformation in Christ*, 2.

[49] *Transformation in Christ*, 4–5.

[50] *Transformation in Christ*, 32–33.

[51] *Transformation in Christ*, 276–78.

[52] *Liturgy and Personality*, 154–55.

Bibliography

The New Tower of Babel (Essays). Manchester, NH: Sophia Institute Press, 1994.

Liturgy and Personality. Manchester, NH: Sophia Institute Press, 1986.

Man and Woman. Chicago: Franciscan Herald Press, 1966.

Transformation in Christ: On the Christian Attitude of Mind. San Francisco: Ignatius Press, 2001.

The Art of Living. Chicago: Franciscan Herald Press, 1994.

The Heart: An Analysis of Human and Divine Affectivity. South Bend: St. Augustine's Press, 2007.

Ethics. Chicago: Franciscan Herald Press, 1972.

Die Metaphysik der Gemeinschaft (The Metaphysics of Community). Regensburg: Verlag Josef Habbel, 1975. Excerpt translated by John F. Crosby.

Das Wesen der Liebe (The Nature of Love). Regensburg: Verlag Josef Habbel, 1971. Excerpt translated by John F. Crosby. Translation of entire work forthcoming, St. Augustine's Press.

In Defense of Purity. Chicago: Franciscan Herald Press, 1970.

Marriage: The Mystery of Faithful Love. Manchester, NH: Sophia Institute Press, 1997.

Der Christliche Ständestaat (*The Christian Corporative State*), "Masse und Gemeinschaft," January 12, 1936, in *Memoiren und Aufsätze gegen den Nationalsozialismus* (*Memoirs and Essays against National Socialism*), ed. by Ernst Wenisch (Mainz: Matthias-Grünewald-Verlag, 1994), 315–18. Excerpt translated by Mary K. Seifert and John Henry Crosby. Translation of entire volume forthcoming, 2007.

Dietrich von Hildebrand Legacy Project

The *Dietrich von Hildebrand Legacy Project* was founded to engage contemporary thought and culture by promoting the thought and spirit of Dietrich von Hildebrand, especially in the English-speaking world.

Pope John Paul II and Pope Benedict XVI have both called for the renewal of Christian philosophy, and the writings of Dietrich von Hildebrand are a remarkable anticipation of these calls. In his now-famous Regensburg address, Pope Benedict lamented the modern "self-limitation of reason" and exhorted philosophers and theologians to have the "courage to engage the whole breadth of reason and not [to deny] . . . its grandeur." Von Hildebrand's prolific writings on metaphysics, ethics, aesthetics, political philosophy, love, marriage, and so forth represent just the kind of courageous engagement of the "whole of reason" envisioned by Pope Benedict.

Pope Benedict is a special admirer of von Hildebrand and a friend of the Legacy Project. Prior to his elevation to the papacy, he joined the Legacy Project as an Honorary Member; yet even as pope, his support has been concrete and vital. Pope Benedict recently gave a striking assessment of von Hildebrand's stature:

I am personally convinced that, when, at some time in the future, the intellectual history of the Catholic Church in the twentieth century is written, the name of Dietrich von Hildebrand will be most prominent among the figures of our time.

The Legacy Project seeks to unleash the power of von Hildebrand's writings for a new generation of readers by translating and publishing his German writings into English; by bringing his many English writings back into print; by engaging in targeted distribution and dissemination of these publications; by hosting conferences and events to facilitate the human reception of his thought; by collecting and preserving the remembrances of von Hildebrand by those who knew him; by publishing a quarterly newsletter, called *Transformation*; and by developing the definitive von Hildebrand website.

For more information on Dietrich von Hildebrand and the Legacy Project, please visit us at www.hildebrandlegacy.org.

Jules van Schaijik

Jules van Schaijik was born and raised in The Netherlands. Originally planning a career in business, his interest in philosophy was awakened at Franciscan University of Steubenville through the encounter with Dietrich von Hildebrand's thought in the areas of love, marriage, and ethics. After graduating in 1988, he and his wife, Katie, studied together at the International Academy of Philosophy in Liechtenstein under Josef Seifert, John Crosby, and Rocco Buttiglione, where their commitment to personalist philosophy—especially as it is found in the work of such thinkers as von Hildebrand, Søren Kierkegaard, John Henry Newman, and Karol Wojtyla—grew and deepened. He received his doctorate in 2001 and taught at Ave Maria University for five years. He and his wife are co-founders of the fledgling Center for Christian Personalism in West Chester, PA. His appreciation for and dedication to von Hildebrand's legacy continues to grow, in part through close friendship and intellectual collaboration with von Hildebrand's widow, Alice von Hildebrand, who spends summers in New Hampshire with the van Schaijiks and their five children.

Index